How To Win Client's & Influence People

CREATE INSTANT CREDIBILITY AND GAIN AN UNFAIR ADVANTAGE OVER YOUR COMPETITION

By Andy Buyting
International Bestselling Author
CarlePublishing.com

♦♦♦

FREE Recorded Message

Reading this book will change
your business! Call now to hear an
important Free Recorded Message from
Andy Buyting at **(800) 819 2804!**

Content

Forward

By Verne Harnish

In 1885, John Deere did something revolutionary – they created their own branded-magazine, The Furrow. Not only did the magazine provide true value to the reader through their educational articles, but it was also the first company-branded magazine in a time when merely 3,500 magazines were in circulation*.

By publishing The Furrow, John Deere was able to own the ink in their industry, positioning themselves as a thought leader in the marketplace.

One-hundred and thirty-two years later, start up, Dollar Shave Club has captured 51% of the online razor industry (compared to Gillette's 21%) and as a result, Unilever purchased the business for $1 billion in 2017. One of the keys to Dollar Shave Club's success is their ability to own the ink though videos that clearly identifies with their buyer.

For years I have been challenging entrepreneurs to own the ink, by writing a book, magazine, blog, video, and more.

When Andy Buyting, an entrepreneur, latched onto the idea, it was completely unexpected.

To leverage the concept of owning the ink, Andy transitioned his retail garden center's antiquated newsletter into a branded magazine. That magazine dubbed *Green Village Home & Garden* became his firm's top lead generator, and enabled repeat purchases from clients.

Like John Deere and Dollar Shave Club, Andy was able to position his firm as a thought leader in the marketplace and as a result, he created an unfair advantage over his competition.

Today, Andy and his team at Carle Publishing help businesses gain the same competitive advantages that he had created for his former garden center firm.

Whether you are leveraging print marketing, digital marketing, or events, entrepreneurs should always seek to own the ink and thereby own the industry. Do you own the ink in your industry?

*There were 3,500 magazines in circulation by 1900 http://www.themagazinist.com/uploads/Part_1_Population_and_Literacy.pdf

Chapter One

The Original Magazine

"Whoever owns the ink in an industry controls the industry." – Verne Harnish

"Andy – whoever owns the ink in their industry controls the industry. Do you own the ink?" stated Verne Harnish, *New York Times* Best Selling Author and authority of fast-growth organizations.

Seated at the MIT Endicott House as part of MIT's three-year program, Birthing of Giants (BOG), with 60 other fast-growth entrepreneurs, I listened raptly to each speaker who took the podium. During one of the evening socials, I pulled Verne aside to discuss my family business and my yearning to "take it to the next level."

Green Village Home & Garden, my family business, was a retail home and garden center on the east coast. After running the business for four years, I had managed to grow sales by over 150% and we were gearing up to open a second retail location. The problem was, even with strong sales, I found myself in a constant struggle competing with big box retailers like Wal-Mart, Costco and Home Depot – it was time to shake things up.

"Do you own the ink?" Verne inquired. "Why don't you consider publishing a set of gardening books or a magazine?"

Verne's advice opened my eyes and allowed me to not only drastically scale my family business, but also become the authority in my marketplace. Working with my marketing team, we replaced our long-standing newsletter we published for over a decade and implemented a quarterly magazine dubbed *Green Village Home & Garden Magazine.* Our magazine influenced what our customers were reading and branded *Green Village Home & Garden* as a dominant market leader.

Our first issues were hugely successful and well-received by our customers. It was official – *Green Village Home & Garden* was now in publishing and we owned the ink in our industry.

When other garden centers across the country started to take notice, I knew I was onto a concept that could not only help my family business grow and own the ink, but other businesses as well.

Realizing the opportunity, I created a customized magazine program and presented it to a group of 20 operators. My idea was to get four-to-six stores signed onto the magazine program, and move forward with a business centered on the concept. That day, I left the meeting with 12 purchase orders in hand. In 2012, Carle Publishing Inc. was incorporated and I made that business my full-time focus.

Our debut issue was so successful that we went to press with a print and distribution run of 280,000 magazines across Canada – outperforming the country's premier garden magazine with a circulation 130% larger.

During our first year of business, we were approached by our insurance agency who asked if we could create a branded business magazine to promote its commercial insurance business. Then, not too shortly after, came the healthcare providers, home builders, wealth managers, lawyers, manufacturers, business consultants, IT and just about every other type of business.

Just as the original *Green Village Home & Garden Magazine* allowed our family business to own the ink and influence our audience, so can specific marketing practices allow you to own the ink and create and dominate your industry; which is why at Carle Publishing, our purpose (or mission) is – "enable our Client-Partners to differentiate and become the authority in their marketplace."

This book is based off my experiences as an entrepreneur and the experience of the entrepreneurial firms that use Carle Publishing to own the ink in their industry.

Chapter Two

The Truth About Thought Leadership

You are a thought leader in your industry, whether you realize it or not.

"The key to success: Know what you know, know you know what you know and be known for what you know." – Author Unknown

OUT-READ TO OUT-LEARN YOUR COMPETITION

After starting Carle Publishing and transitioning from our family-owned garden center to running a business-to-business enterprise, I quickly realized that I not only did not understand the publishing world, but I did not understand sales.

That is when I began devouring sales books written by Jack Daly, Chet Holmes, Jeffrey Gitomer, Daniel Pink, Bill Bishop, Simon Sinek, Nick Nanton, Dean Walton, Dan Goldberg, Brent Adamson and Matthew Dixon, among other authorities. Twelve months later, after dedicating time to learn about sales, I had easily caught up with 90% of the people in the industry – essentially making myself an expert. Being an avid reader is crucial to furthering your expertise. Perhaps author Earl Nightingale said it best when he wrote, "Reading one hour per day in your chosen field will make you an international expert in seven years."

According to a study conducted by the Pew Research Center, 26% of adults said they had not read any books within the past year. Instead, they relied on experience – based learning. And while experience-based learning is crucial, it is table stakes – your competitor has the same experience.

Did you know that countless successful men and women today and throughout history have been avid readers? Mark Cuban, owner of the NBA's Mavericks and a shark from ABC's reality television series, Shark Tank, spends three hours a day reading. Mark Zuckerberg, founder of Facebook, reads two business books per month. Nike founder, Phil Knight, is such a lover of books that upon entering his library, you have to take your shoes off and bow.

So, what's the takeaway? Everyone should be out-reading and out-learning their competition.

THE TRUTH ABOUT THOUGHT LEADERSHIP

The truth is, that in reality, you are probably already an expert. If you have been working in your industry for five-to-ten years, compared to the rest of the population, you are an expert. Whether you have been selling insurance for 10 years or own and run a small plumbing company, you know something that 99% of the population does not know.

However, to become a true elite industry expert, to be someone who has more than just experience-based learning, you need to pick up a book and start reading. Once you do, it is not difficult to become an industry expert, or even an elite within your industry. The difficult part? Finding a way to market your expertise so that the world values your knowledge and authority.

Throughout the chapters of this book, we will focus on solving this marketing challenge through the three pillars of marketing, which include:

PILLAR ONE: ONLINE DIGITAL MARKETING

Leveraging online marketing to get your brand out to the marketplace in multiple formats is effective and is easier than you think. Yet, having a good online presence is something that must be strategized and well-thought-out.

PILLAR TWO: PRINT MARKETING

Print is not dead. In fact, print is perceived as having more status and credibility than online marketing. Utilizing modern-day methods of print marketing is a big win to establish your brand authority.

PILLAR THREE: INTERACTIVE MARKETING

At the end of the day, a clever tweet or a well-thought-out book will not make sales. Potential clients need access to the first two pillars, but in the end, for most of us, people are needed to close a sale. Interactive marketing includes interactions between the buyer and the seller, whether it be face-to-face interactions, events, webinars or phone calls, these are all forms of interactive marketing.

Someone once said that the key to success was, "Know what you know. Know you know what you know. Be known for what you know."

And you know what? You already know what you know, whether you are a home builder that has built houses for several years, or an entrepreneur that has survived the start-up phase, you know something unique that most people do not. The next step is to continue learning and leverage that knowledge to grow your business by being known for what you know.

Chapter Three

Why Most Cultures Look to Published Authors as Thought Leaders

---

"The more that you read, the more things you will know. The more things that you learn, the more places you will go." – Dr. Seuss

Even after publishing our quarterly magazine, I knew that to stay top-of-mind and continue to appeal to a larger audience, I needed to leverage my knowledge using multiple channels. In 2007, after publishing the book, *The Retailer's Roadmap to Success,* which shared my knowledge of how to compete with big-name competitors like Home Depot and Wal-Mart, a demand for keynote presentations drastically increased. It was then that *Green Village Home & Garden* was seen as the authority in the retail industry.

As an added bonus – we generated a small profit from publishing the book through book sales and paid speaking engagements.

WHY DID PUBLISHING MY BOOK INSPIRE A DEMAND INCREASE FOR KEYNOTE PRESENTATIONS?

In a Huffington Post article, Chuck Boyce, CEO of Authority Media Group once stated that the word authority begins with author, meaning that if you have written a book, created your own branded magazine, or simply written a column in a local paper, then you have expert status in your field of choice.

Because I published a book on the subject, event organizers and sponsors saw me as the *authority* in the independent retail industry.

Additionally, according to a Wesley Hills Group survey of over 200 business book authors, "The vast majority of authors surveyed – 96% – realized a significant positive impact on their business from writing a book and would recommend the practice."

Whether you are an expert or not, being a published author provides you the instant credibility needed to market to your audience and be *known for what you know.*

UTILIZING PRINT TO BUILD YOUR BRAND'S PERCEIVED EXPERTISE

Guy Maddalone, CEO of GTM, a payroll services business, has also reaped the benefits of *owning the ink in his industry.* After publishing his book *How to Hire and Retain Your Household Help,* he was able to cement himself and GTM as industry experts and increased his revenue.

After two-and-a-half years and 7,000 copies, Guy reports, "A couple Fortune 500 companies have purchased copies and then hired me as a speaker for lunch and learns," which has led him to acquire multiple new customers. Additionally, he has appeared on several New York television shows and in articles in the *Wall Street Journal* and *New York Times.*

Steve Kearley, founder of Benson Kearley IFG, a Toronto-based insurance agency, found that publishing a bi-annual custom branded business magazine increased his firm's credibility; he says, "Publishing our own magazine has been very good for Benson Kearley IFG. The publication has helped establish our brand in the greater Toronto marketplace and positions our firm as a thought leader in the industry."

Due to their increased credibility in the market, their sales process improved. Before publishing the magazine, sales personnel would receive two out of 10 meetings pitched. "It wasn't a bad batting average for the industry," explains Kearley, "However, by affirming our credibility in the region through our magazine, our average has increased to eight out of ten."

For Dr. Charles Mok, owner of Allure Medical Spa, a Detroit-based medical spa, he sought to publish a magazine to enhance his credibility when engaging with prospects, and to reaffirm his relationships with customers.

After distributing 20,000 copies of his first issue to existing customers, and 30,000 to prospects, he received over 2,000 appointments directly from the recipients of his magazine within six weeks, generating $386,000 in revenue. Today, Dr. Mok issues an Allure-branded magazine regularly.

IT TAKES MORE THAN JUST PRINT

What sets really exceptional thought leaders apart from the rest, is that exceptional thought leaders know how to leverage the content that they produce. By using multiple mediums, they own the ink in the industry they serve through books, magazines, blogs, videos, podcasts and more.

Take legendary wine shop owner turned marketing guru Gary Vaynerchuck, who, in 2006, created a YouTube vlog (video + blog) called *Wine Library TV* featuring wine advice and reviews in his "unique, down-to-earth yet bombastic style." Eventually, the show reached cult status and Gary began receiving calls from news outlets looking to interview "the internet wine guy."

By leveraging his digital media expertise to publish the book, "Crush It" in 2009, coupled with his vlog, he is one of the most in-demand keynote speakers in the United States.

According to Maili Wong, First Vice President of The Wong Group, a boutique investment and financial advisory firm, "By publishing a magazine and book, plus a blog and video content, I've been able to establish The Wong Group as a market leader in the Vancouver region."

In addition to publishing their branded magazine called *Smart Risk Magazine*, Wong also published *Smart Risk: Investing Like the Wealthy to Achieve a Work-Optional Life*, which became an Amazon bestseller. She also started video podcasting and writing a weekly blog. As a result, Wong appeared on radio talk shows like CNBC Radio and Business in Vancouver Roundhouse Radio and was even chosen to give a TEDx talk, which surpassed 3,000 views.

Chapter Four

Get Their Attention!

A good marketing strategy begins with the buyer.

"Treat your customers like they own you. Because they do." – Mark Cuban

What is 51% of the razor industry worth? For Unilever, $1 billion.

In 2017, Unilever paid Dollar Shave Club for the privilege to own the start-up that had then overtaken former entrant Gillette. But Unilever was not paying Dollar Shave Club for just a good razor, they were purchasing a corner of the *male grooming market* with a tight-knit group of buyers who provide quick feedback loops on new products.

In 2012, no company could compete with Gillette in the razor industry; they owned 72% of the U.S. marketing share. And yet, on March 6, 2012, the YouTube video *DollarShaveClub - Our Razors or F***ing Awesome* was released and took off, instantly going viral. By 2016, Dollar Shave Club claimed 51% of the online market compared with Gillette's 21%.

For CEO and founder Mike Dubin, *razors were just the beginning…* "American men are evolving in their bathroom routine," says Dubin in an interview with *Entrepreneur Magazine*. "Five years ago, if you spent time in front of the mirror, people would have called you 'metrosexual'. We now live in the age where it's OK to hug guys and compliment and give advice."

They have since expanded their product portfolio to encompass additional male grooming products like hair and skin care products. They are even considering creating male makeup, a product Dollar Shave Club is convinced the American male is on the cusp of accepting.

Why was Dollar Shave Club a success? It is not just the witty viral YouTube videos and clever packaging. Dollar Shave Club understands their Core Customer and focuses on serving that buyer.

So, who is their customer? Twenty-somethings who are on the search for the ideal razor without the price tag that comes paired with big brand names. While their customer wants to come across as being a "manly man," he has lots of questions about grooming that he may not feel comfortable addressing with friends or peers.

The focus on their Core Customer translates to all of Dollar Shave Club's marketing. For example, blog article titles include:

Here's How to Shave with Acne Prone Skin
How to Stop Eating Everything That's in Front of You
The Number of Shirt Buttons That's Acceptable to Leave Unbuttoned
Should I be Moisturizing my You-Know-What?

By understanding their Core Customer, Dollar Shave Club is able to market most effectively by utilizing messaging that specifically attracts and *eventually* converts prospects.

IT ALL BEGINS WITH THE BUYER

There are three components to creating an effective marketing strategy – identifying your Core Customer (your ideal buyer), understanding the buying cycle, and deciding on your message and medium. The first component, identifying your Core Customer, is one Dollar Shave Club intimately understands but few other businesses do.

When I started working at my family business, I was intuitively attracted to marketing and how businesses promoted themselves. At one of the many conferences I attended, I remember hearing from a speaker whose message really impacted me.

He explained that businesses spend extensive time and energy in selecting the right medium to advertise to their market – but when it came down to actually writing the content, those same businesses would leave it to the advertising company's "creative team" with very little thought to the effectiveness of the message itself. In other words, they labor over what radio station they should be on, or which page they should appear within the local newspaper, but when it came to the message they deliver, they would simply tell the advertising firm to do it for them.

If this sounds like you, you may believe you are making the right decisions by focusing on the medium, or "how" you are going to reach your target audience. However, by not prioritizing your message, you receive a bad return on your investment because you simply are not deliberate in creating the right message that will inspire your audience to take action. You might be reaching your audience, but the message is not making a difference. This is why it is crucial that you know your buyer inside and out so that you can identify and create the right messaging to sell your business' products or services.

Management guru Peter Drucker echoes the same sentiment, "The aim of marketing is to know and understand the customer so well the product or service fits him and sells itself."

IDENTIFYING YOUR CORE CUSTOMER

Many companies describe their Core Customers through the use of a Customer Avatar – or a semi-fictional representation of the ideal customer based on market research and data on your existing customer base. It includes demographics, likes and dislikes, goals, buying patterns, language and more. These data help companies determine how to best attract the most valuable prospects and potential customers.

In his book *The Inside Advantage*, Dr. Robert Bloom discusses the importance of identifying your Core Customer. According to Dr. Bloom, every business should write a detailed 25-word narrative outlining their Core Customer; he even suggests giving your Core Customer a name. By articulating this persona, Dr. Bloom reports that companies focus their market strategy to include the proper message on the proper mediums to target that customer.

SEVENTEEN MAGAZINE

In the early days of *Seventeen Magazine*, its management team was looking for a way to pitch the magazine to businesses in hopes to advertise their products on their pages. In an effort to explain their reader (Core Customer), promotion director Estelle Ellis created a customer avatar named *Teena* based on surveys of teenage girls and their mothers.

Here is their description from Kelley Massoni's book *Fashioning Teenagers: A Cultural History of Seventeen Magazine*

> Teena the High School Girl has a peck of problems. She's what older folks call an awkward adolescent—too tall, too plump, too shy—a little too much of a lot of little things. But they're big things to Teena. And though she doesn't always take her troubles to mother, Teena writes her favorite magazine for the tip-off on the clothes she wears, the food she eats, the lipstick she wields, the room she bunks in, the budget she keeps, the boy she has a crush on. *Seventeen* seems to have all the answers—that's why like Teena, smart advertisers use *Seventeen*.

The result: advertisers and articles focused on helping *Teena* overcome her insecurities. For example, on one of the early covers, stories listed include: Dates (How to get) and Your Future (Where is it?).

PAINTER PROS' CORE CUSTOMER

Painter Pros, a painting business that focuses on supplying quality interior home painting, has a customer avatar, called *Momma Mary*. She is a working mother between 30 to 45 years old, and has little-to-no time to do any large projects around the house because she works full time and spends time with her family on weekends. She is also tech savvy and loves to interact on social media. Efficiency and time management are crucial to *Momma Mary*, as she has a limited window to bring in contractors while still being able to oversee the job. She is hands on, organized and detail oriented.

So, with all of these details, Painter Pros understands that *Momma Mary* is most concerned with spending time with her family, and will in turn provide her with an efficient, well-organized painting job.*

THE BUYING CYCLE

Now that you have established your Core Customer and are able to develop effective marketing collateral that best meets their needs, how do you ensure that you get the phone call, meeting or visit you need to close the sale?

When it comes to marketing and selling your products or services, it takes more than just one touch to attract and convert leads. Your expectations should never be that someone will see your advertisement or read a blog post and immediately make a purchase; it is much more involved than that. It takes several marketing touches and/or sales touches to solidify the deal. According to Salesforce.com, it takes six to eight touches before a prospect turns into a viable sales lead – let alone converting that lead into a buyer.

In fact, there is an inherent process known as the buying cycle that attracts prospects, nurtures them and turns those prospects into buyers.

The chart below outlines a typical buying cycle. Let us take a moment to explore each step.

1. AWARENESS AD AND NEED
It all starts with an awareness ad or message. Without a potential awareness and need of your product or service, your message will not even get off of home plate in the mind of your potential customer. If you are an estate planner and a fourteen-year-old boy sees your advertisement, it will fall on deaf ears as they are not even close to your Core Customer.

However, if your estate planning advertisement is seen by an aging parent in his golden years, there is a good chance that they will enter the buying cycle.

2. SOCIAL INFLUENCE
Through social influence, you are causing the buyer to think about your product or service by keeping it front of mind. For example, your prospect thinks about estate planning when he looks at his children, or when he hears his friends discuss estate planning for their families.

Marketing can influence your buyer's thinking when you produce content that is important to the buyer. For example, perhaps your buyer is reading about friends who are considering estate planning based on what they are sharing on Facebook – maybe it was a blog he came across and read that your company published.

Knowing what your buyer is thinking about, his wife may share an article that she saw in a magazine – an article that you wrote about how to get started with estate planning.

3. PERSONAL CONSIDERATION

After gaining validation through social influence, your prospect then starts to internalize his thinking about whether it is the right purchase for him to consider, does he need estate planning, and when is the right time. Prospects that make it to this stage in your buying cycle are seriously considering making a purchase of your product or service and want to learn more. They have gone from passively receiving your marketing message to actually researching solutions.

This is where your marketing strategy can really help move things along. Once a buyer reaches this stage, your value-added content marketing can go a long way to influence their decision-making process. Once a prospect is starting to look for more information to make a buying decision, you want to ensure that they are receiving your advertising and content – including different mediums: online, in print and, when possible, in person.

4. VALIDATION

No one likes making a bad decision, and so during this stage, your buyer is validating that they are about to make the "right" decision. To influence your buyer at the validation stage, you need to position your brand as the "right" choice. They need to have the ability to trust your company's product or service. For example, during this stage, you might create an educational blog post outlining how some products and services are superior to others, and why, or you might initiate a demo of your product so the buyer can see it in action at no cost or risk to them.

5. PURCHASE

Finally, once you have removed all doubt, your goal is to have that prospect make a purchase decision and become your client.

IT TAKES THE ENTIRE CYCLE TO ATTRACT AND CONVERT A BUYER

Consider the last time you purchased a car – you knowingly or unknowingly went through each stage of the buying cycle before purchasing. Here's a fictional example:

You are sitting in bed scrolling through your Facebook feed when you realize your sister has just purchased a brand-new BMW M3. This causes you to consider your current car and wince inwardly – perhaps you should soon look to upgrade; without being consciously aware, you have entered the social influence stage of the buying cycle.

You think the M3 looks nice and cannot help but remember that magazine ad you saw earlier in the day advertising the latest model, piquing your interest. The next morning, the BMW ad in the newspaper jumps out at you like it has never done before, and you find yourself clicking through their website to read all the features and benefits of the M3 while enjoying your morning coffee. Later that evening, almost without realizing, you find yourself reading about the M3 on an online consumer review board, and when a particular blog post catches your eye, you devour the content – you are now at the personal consideration stage.

Later that week, you run into your sister at the grocery store and listen to her rave about her new M3; she even lets you try it out in the parking lot. You decide that it is time to start looking into the M3 for yourself. You do some online digging about its features and price using BMW's blog and check out the reviews – validation stage. You decide it is in your price range and are seriously interested in checking out the vehicle. After visiting the dealer to get additional questions answered, you take the newest model for a spin. The dealer hands you a copy of a magazine that they published containing informative and entertaining articles about BMW cars. He points out the feature story on the M3. After some consideration, you decide to make a purchase.

Even though that is a simplified example of how a buyer moves through the buying cycle, it clearly demonstrates how each stage within the cycle is important to attract, influence and ultimately convert the prospect into a customer. It also shows how you need all three pillars of marketing to successfully move the customer through the buying cycle.

LEVERAGING THE THREE PILLARS

During each step of the buyer's cycle, your prospect should be receiving "touches" or communications that use the three pillars of marketing: digital, print and interactive marketing.

PILLAR ONE — DIGITAL MARKETING
Digital marketing involves all online forms of marketing including blogging, video, podcasts, social media tools and more. It allows marketers to provide frequent reminders or short messages that keep a brand top of mind.

PILLAR TWO — PRINT MARKETING
Print marketing encompasses all print marketing collateral including catalogs, magazines, books, white papers and sales literature. This type of marketing is crucial because it not only has more credibility than digital, but also has a longer life-span as you are more likely to hang onto printed material

PILLAR THREE — INTERACTIVE MARKETING
Interactive marketing includes face-to-face interactions, phone calls as well as tools such as meetings, presentations and events. It involves situations where you are able to directly interact with potential buyers, and is most often needed to close the deal.

Because every buyer consumes information and content through multiple mediums and each medium serves a slightly different purpose, it is crucial to utilize all three pillars when it comes to communicating to your Core Customer. While they may be more influenced by one pillar over another, each buyer is different. Through compiling data and information from each pillar, you are not only able to keep the message alive in a multitude of ways, but you are able to attract buyers that prefer different methods of communication.

Throughout the next several chapters, we will explore the three pillars in depth and the different tactics and tools you can utilize to leverage your expertise, create instant credibility and gain an unfair advantage over your competition.

Bonus Follow Up Tools

Visit **www.CarlePublishing.com/ Resources** to learn more about building a customer avatar and get access a downloadable template by tapping into Carle Publishing's free resources.

Chapter Five

Busting the Myths of Digital Marketing

It is effective and can be easier than you think!

"The secret of getting ahead is getting started." – Mark Twain

Dean Graziozi had already built a multi-million-dollar real estate business when he realized he could leverage digital marketing, specifically infomercials, to deliver his message on how to make money in real estate to the masses.

Dean is a real estate investor turned best-selling author and inspirational speaker. He is known for his "long running interview style TV shows" (aka his infomercials). In fact, Dean has leveraged infomercials on late night TV since 1999 and has appeared on TV almost daily for nearly 15 years.

It is safe to say that communication comes easily to Dean.

With the advent of social media, Dean recognized the opportunity to spread his word and reach. He adapted his infomercial-style videos to the small, bite-sized videos preferred on YouTube and social media. With over 450 videos and a social reach in the millions, Dean has certainly become a digital marketing powerhouse.

His secret? Creating valuable, yet entertaining digital content through video and articles.

THE POWER OF INBOUND MARKETING

According to an eMarketing Report, consumers today are spending more time online than any other media outlet, including TV, print, radio and the like. Consumers, now more than ever, are using the internet to research solutions for their problems and validate the products and services they are purchasing – which is a crucial part of the buying cycle. It is important that customers are engaged in digital marketing tactics and are receiving the value they seek. This will not only help you acquire leads and close prospects, but it is often easier and cheaper than engaging in other forms of marketing.

With two forms of marketing, outbound and inbound, it is essential that you understand the difference.

Outbound marketing includes paid advertising like Google Adwords, banner ads, telemarketing and social media advertising and is considered "push marketing." In this way, the marketer is according to Hubspot, "pushing their message out far and wide hoping that it resonates with that needle in the haystack." This method is inefficient and does not create value to consumers, and Hubspot reports that outbound marketing costs 62% more than inbound marketing techniques.

Inbound marketing in contrast provides value-added, education-driven content to consumers and includes blogs, video, podcasts, white papers and more. By providing valuable, educational content to consumers, you position your brand as a thought leader in the industry.

According to the 2017 State of Inbound Report by HubSpot, 46% of the professionals surveyed said inbound marketing generated a higher ROI than outbound marketing and 59% indicated that inbound supplies higher quality leads than outbound.

The common theme here? There is power behind inbound marketing.

WAYS PEOPLE CONSUME CONTENT ONLINE

There are four primary ways people consume content online – through written articles, written listicles, videos and audio forms.

Throughout the remainder of the chapter, we will explore each of these methods, how they help businesses grow and ways to easily start incorporating them into your marketing arsenal.

WEEDPRO LAWN CARE WINS WITH THE WRITTEN FORM

WeedPro Lawn Care in Columbus, Ohio began turning toward inbound marketing in 2012 to generate and convert leads. Through their numerous inbound marketing tactics, they reported a 230% growth rate year over year.

According to Shaun Kanary in an interview with Hubspot, "Our blogs and white papers have led to better qualified leads and actual sales."

As WeedPro quickly became recognized as the authority in lawn care industry, they were even picked up by a leading industry magazine and featured in a four-page spread on their innovative inbound marketing strategy – leading to even more exposure.

It is no wonder blogs and whitepapers have led Shaun to develop qualified leads when according to an eMarketing report, websites with a blog tend to have 434% more indexed pages than websites without a blog; thus, websites with a blog rank higher and have a better opportunity of making the first three pages of Google than pages without a blog. That is because Google – like the consumer – prefers websites with a wide diversity of helpful content.

WRITTEN ARTICLES - HOW DO YOU GET STARTED?

You do not always need an IT specialist to add a blog to your website; it is actually quite easy. But if adding a blog does not work for you, or you do not want your blog associated with your website, writing articles on your LinkedIn page is a great alternative for providing educational content to your consumers.

Creating white papers, and enticing prospects to download it in exchange for providing their personal information, is another valuable method of incorporating the written form into your marketing strategy.

If it works so well, what is keeping more people from writing blogs or creating white papers? The answer is often a lack of time. If you are like most entrepreneurs and marketing managers, you may not have the time needed to create a weekly or monthly blog post. The good news is, there are freelance websites like MediaBistro, Reedsy, UpWork and Fiverr that can provide quality ghostwriters at a reasonable cost.

WRITTEN LISTICLES

Conductor, a marketing platform, performed a survey of headline preferences for articles. The headlines ranged from numbered, reader addressing, how to, questions and normal. Can you guess which headline type outperformed the others?

Numbered headlines – winning at 36%.

Numbered headlines are often described as listicles or list posts; they are easily spotted by their titles – "The six ways to be more productive at your office" or "The seven habits highly successful people do every morning."

They are extremely effective, as the reader can scan the headlines and read only the details on concepts and points that pique their interest. And with the ever-increasing demand on people's time, listicles have quickly become a preferred way to consume the written word online.

Many businesses and authorities use listicles, proving that they have value and are popular. From Hubspot – where 4 of 7 blog articles posted are listicles, to BuzzFeed – a content curator whose entire model is based off listicles, to Kevin Daum, marketing consultant and Inc.com contributor, that prefers listicles to nearly any other article form, listicles reign supreme.

MISSOURI STAR QUILTING CO. UTILIZES VIDEO TO GROW THEIR BUSINESS

Cisco Visual Networking Index forecast states, "Internet video will account for 79% of global internet traffic by 2020." Video's importance in the buying cycle is growing, and is becoming a powerful way to provide content because when consumers are viewing information through video, they are more likely to give it their full attention.

The Doan family utilized video to build their business, Missouri Star Quilting Co., when during the recession, Ron Doan (father) lost a huge chunk of his retirement savings in the market crash. The family leveraged Donna Doan's (mother) flair for the dramatic and love for quilting to create a YouTube channel.

Today, their YouTube channel has over 400,000 subscribers, and generates traffic to their website – pulling in annual revenues of over $20 million. What does this prove? Video works.

VIDEO - HOW DO YOU GET STARTED?

While I prefer video that is two to three minutes in length, various video-marketing authorities quote different ideal time lengths. Nick Nanton, author of Amazon Bestseller, *Story Selling*, believes that there is no such thing as a video that is too long. When a potential customer says your video is too long, they are really saying that your video is not engaging.

I do believe that the more valuable and entertaining your content is, the less video length is an issue. However, I still believe that in today's busy world, not many people have time to watch ten minutes worth of video.

Not sure how to get started? There are two ways you can produce videos. You can either hire a videographer to help you plan, shoot and edit your videos professionally or you can create them in-house. Although professionally produced videos are nice to have, when it comes to producing regular content for your audience, I am a big fan of creating videos yourself. In our company, we use professionals to produce core anchor videos (six to eight videos in total), however, when creating our vlogs (video blogs) to share content regularly, we produce them all in-house.

Creating videos in-house may seem like a complicated endeavor, however, it can be easier than you think. By utilizing freelance sites to find an editor for your videos, your job is simply to film.

To create a great video in-house, there are three core pieces of equipment that you will want to have. These three pieces of equipment will take care of most quality issues that might make your videos feel "amateur-ish" or homemade. They include:

1. **A high-definition video webcam.** You can use your laptop or smartphone, however, I recommend spending the money to get a high-definition webcam that plugs into your computer. It is well worth the investment.

2. **A lapel microphone to ensure professional audio quality.** When you watch a video that does not seem professional, it is often the sound quality that is giving it that feeling. A basic lapel microphone will make a world of a difference in your sound quality, eliminating the echoing sound that we too often hear in videos.

3. **Umbrella lighting or a desktop light.** When you are on camera, you want

the lighting to be on you. This does not need to be a complicated production. With a simple desktop light, you can have good lighting and prevent any unwanted shadows across your face by your office lighting or a nearby window.

The total investment needed for the three items listed can be as low as $300 to $400.

With the right equipment in hand, you are ready to start shooting. Do not make it complicated. Simply plug in your equipment and use the standard recording app that comes with your operating system to start recording your content.

You may be asking yourself, "What do I record and how do I get started?" Well, that all depends on what you want to try and accomplish with your videos. I suggest you start with a plan of what value you want your video to deliver to your audience and what action you want the consumer to take as a result of watching it. I love using regular vlogs to share updates, tips and other value-added content with my audiences.

To maximize your video's effectiveness, you will want to have it structured in a way that it is both to-the-point and entertaining. Below is a video outline that is recommended by video blogging guru James Wedmore:

1. **Attention Grabber (2-6 seconds)** — Reveal the benefit of the video or a teaser of what's to come: "Today we are talking about the [introduce subject matter]."
2. **Intro Bumper (4-7 seconds)** — Animate your logo with a strong sound bed to set the tone. You can have one generated on Fiverr or UpWork.
3. **The Content (1-5 minutes)** — Deliver the content you promised in a concise and clear manner. End this section by including a call to action for the viewer so they continue down the buying cycle.
4. **Outro Bumper (4-7 seconds)** – Bring in your animated logo and text to deliver your call to action.
5. **Outtakes (4-7 seconds)** — Including bloopers is a fun way to end a video and stir up some laughs. This makes the video entertaining for the prospect to watch right to the end.

Your Youtube Video Template

Credit: James Wedmore

GREENFEET.COM BUILDS BRAND EVANGELISTS WITH PODCASTS

An eco-friendly e-commerce retailer, GreenFeet.com, faced issues connecting with customers. Valerie Reddermann, founder and president of GreenFeet.com, says that podcasting has allowed them to connect with customers worldwide and has created "brand evangelists."

"They become extremely enthusiastic," explains Redderman in an interview with Mashable. "They really connect with the company and they understand that we're more than just a company…These are people who I find…that mention our names to family and friends, that talk about us on their blogs, that tweet about us."

Audio content, including podcast and free recorded messages, is an often-overlooked area of digital marketing – but it is currently disrupting the way society consumes content. As an example, in 2017 Edison Research reported that 24% of Americans ages 12 and up have listened to a podcast in the past month – that is the same number of Americans on Twitter.

One of the reasons for this is because a podcast is the easiest form of content to consume. Unlike video that requires your full attention, podcasts can be digested while driving, going for a walk or when doing menial tasks.

PODCASTS - HOW DO YOU GET STARTED?

When it comes to podcasting, there are different ways you can create content. One of the most popular forms is by interviewing others, essentially creating a "radio show" and publishing it as a podcast.

Another popular format is by simply doing a one-way dialogue, which includes sharing knowledge with your audience. If you are already creating videos, this second format can be done with very little added work – simply have a freelance audio editor strip the audio from your video and edit/process it for podcasting.

If you are not currently recording videos, simply download a recording app on your smartphone and regularly record content on various topics that you feel your audience would enjoy. Then, send it to a freelance podcast editor from UpWork or Fiverr to edit and process the recording for you.
Similar to video creation, I suggest using a lapel microphone to ensure good sound quality.

Incorporating free recorded messages is another excellent tool to use in your marketing strategy. According to Joe Polish, speaker and author of *The Average Joe's Marketing Book*, there are three core benefits to using free recorded messages:

1. It enables prospective customers to learn more about your products or services and opt-in to continuing down your sales process. This automatically eliminates those that aren't interested in what you have to offer, and provides a list of ready-to-buy or nearly-ready-to-buy leads.
2. You do not have to worry about having a big ad budget. Free recorded messages are cheap in comparison to most marketing techniques and can often be customized based on budget.
3. Prospects can access a free recorded message 24 hours a day. Even when your sales team is done for the day, your robotic free recorded message is still accessible.

Just how effective are free recorded messages? In 2009, when Joe Polish first started using Twitter, he included a free recorded message on his Twitter page and closed his first deal within his first week. These messages work for Joe and countless other companies and can help yours too.

Creating and using free recorded messages is easy and cheap. Simply record your message on a recording app from your smartphone and host it using platforms like GrassHopper.com, Ka1l8.com or TollFreeForwarding.com. Again, do not forget your lapel microphone for good sound quality.

REMEMBER - YOU ARE AN EXPERT!

If you are nervous about getting started, don't be! With your years of specialization (coupled with your willingness to educate yourself beyond experience-based education), you are already an authority in your industry. Through your ability to understand the pitfalls and opportunities in your industry, you are not only able to harness digital marketing, but also become the thought leader.

Chapter Six

Building and Nurturing Customer and Client Relationships Using Digital Marketing

---

"Get closer than ever to your customers. So close that you tell them what they need well before they realize it themselves." – Steve Jobs

As an entrepreneur or marketer, you understand the importance of leveraging and utilizing digital marketing to reach (1) external customers (current clients and prospective customers), and (2) internal customers (employees). Throughout this chapter, we will discuss how to leverage digital marketing to grow and nurture relationships with external customers.

TWO TYPES OF EXTERNAL CUSTOMERS

There are two types of external customers to consider: prospective customers and current clients.

While the basic toolset for addressing both types of customers is the same, the message may vary drastically. The difference aligns with the classic *Hunting vs. Farming* mentality. If you are targeting prospective customers, the message requires you to include a compelling reason for them to do business with you. On the other hand, when targeting current clients, you need to offer valuable content geared to either retain them as a client or upsell them on additional products and services. Marketing to clients is about nurturing, whereas marketing to potential customers is focused on hunting and reeling in new clients.

As an entrepreneur looking to grow their business, marketing to new customers may seem attractive but in fact, often nurturing or farming current clients can generate a higher return on investment. According to an HBR article titled *The Value of Keeping the Right Customers*, existing clients spend 31% more than new customers and increasing customer retention by 5% increases profits by 25-95%.

WHAT IS A DIGITAL MARKETING STRATEGY?

Regardless of whether you aim to market to prospective customers or current clients, the basic strategy remains consistent: establish who your core customer is, create a message for that core customer and select the ideal vehicle to deliver that message.

NESBIT INSURANCE AGENCY HUNTS FOR NEW CUSTOMERS

Nesbit Insurance Agency is a firm that has clearly nailed each of the three steps in the digital marketing strategy to hunt for new customers.

Located in Minnesota, Nesbit offers commercial insurance to midsize businesses that average over 20 employees. However, Nesbit's Core Customer is not a business; instead it is a CFO. After all, as Bryan Kramar, Social Media Strategist, states, "There's no such thing as B2B or B2C; it's H2H or Human to Human."

Nesbit's Core Customer, CFO Charlie, is risk averse, extremely busy and is looking for a way to maximize his budget. That is why Nesbit's marketing messages are focused on providing content to educate CFO Charlie on how commercial insurance is a strategic component of a good business. Nesbit also understands that CFO Charlie needs to have his online content delivered in two key methods – video and articles, which are sent via email on a monthly basis.

DIVING INTO THE THREE STEPS OF YOUR DIGITAL MARKETING STRATEGY

Step One: Know the Buyer

Before you begin to develop a marketing message, it is crucial that you first establish who your Core Customer is. For a review of what a Core Customer is and how to develop one, visit Chapter Four for a discussion on the subject.

Step Two: What Is the Message?

By utilizing your Core Customer and understanding who they are and what drives them, you are then able to carefully craft your message that will lead them to the next step you want them to take, whatever that may be. This is in fact the most important step, and is often the one that is overlooked.

Ask yourself these three questions – (1) How do I get the attention of my core customers? (2) What value am I adding to their lives? (3) And most importantly, what specific actions do I want them to take after consuming my content? In other words, what is the purpose of your article, video or podcast? And is your messaging achieving your purpose?

Step Three: What Is the Ideal Vehicle to Use?
Once you have crafted the right message, you need to consider the ideal vehicle or tool to deliver the content. With your digital marketing, consider selecting several vehicles to ensure that your buyer has the ability to digest your content in several different ways depending on their preference (written, video and/or audio).

AMERICAN EXPRESS UTILIZES DIGITAL CONTENT TO BUILD CLIENT PARTNER LOYALTY
OpenForum.com is a platform for American Express customers that provides content featuring *"insights, inspiration and connections to help get business done."* It was American Express' way of providing value to their clients – specifically the small business owner – and staying connected in order to retain loyalty.

According to Compete.com, monthly traffic to OpenForum has grown to over 1 million and today, their Twitter following is over 200,000 followers.

American Express is not the only one that is utilizing content to build client loyalty; according to Content Marketing Institute, "64% of B2B marketers say they use content marketing to achieve customer retention and loyalty goals."

Chapter Seven

Using Digital Marketing to Nurture Employee Relationships and Build Culture

The next big opportunity for most businesses!

"Corporate culture is the only sustainable competitive advantage within the control of the entrepreneur." – David Cummings, Co-Founder of Pardot

As far as careers go, working at a call center has a very poor reputation, and it shows. The average turnover rate was about 300%. And the reason why? Operators often make minimal hourly rates and have less-than-convenient hours.

In 2008, Appletree Answers, a call center in New Jersey, had 110% employee turnover. CEO, John Ratliff was often congratulated for exceeding industry standards by colleagues, but John understood that 110% was hurting his bottom line. Ratliff estimated in an interview for an HBR article that "at a cost of $5,000 per turnover, Appletree had a $2.2 million problem – a huge burden for a company generating revenue of just $16 million a year."

Ratliff and his team decided things had to change and they enacted an initiative called Dream On, a concept borrowed from the Make-A-Wish Foundation. "Frontline employees were invited to submit 'dreams' to the executive team, with the promise that some would be chosen and fulfilled."

At first nothing happened – employees thought the initiative was not serious.

Until four weeks later when an employee that had recently gone through a divorce dreamed for an apartment to raise her kids. "They were living in a car," admits John.

Appletree paid her security deposit for the apartment, first and last months' rent and purchased more than $1,000 worth of furniture. According to the HBR article, "The company even promised her landlord that if the employee were to fall behind in payments, Appletree would help."

The employee was absolutely thrilled and word of the Dream On program quickly spread.

Over a period of four years, the company granted 275 dreams with a total investment of roughly $400,000. Employee turnover was reduced from 110% in 2008 to just 30% in 2012.

They started documenting the dreams granted, upon approval of the employee, through video. In fact, video was a huge part of Ratliff's communication strategy across his 23 offices (525 employees). According to Ratliff, "We hired a professional film maker as a fulltime employee. I'm a huge believer that part of what drove our employee turnover way down was how we used videos to create a family atmosphere."

EFFECTIVE EMPLOYEE COMMUNICATION IS A LEADING INDICATOR OF FINANCIAL PERFORMANCE

Just how John Ratliff at Appletree Answers demonstrated, effective and efficient marketing to internal customers – your employees – is a key tactic to strengthening employee engagement.

According to a recent Willis Towers Watson report, "Effective employee communication is a leading indicator of financial performance and a driver of employee engagement. Companies that are highly effective communicators had 47% higher total returns to stakeholders over the past five years compared with firms that are the least effective communicators."

Raj Sisodia, co-founder and co-chairman of Conscious Capitalism Inc., says that, "30% of employees are actively engaged, 52% are not engaged and 18% are actively disengaged." This means disengaged employees represent a $450 to $550 billion a year problem in lost productivity.

In the previous chapter we discussed the two opportunities to leverage when utilizing digital marketing – one being marketing to external customers and clients, and two being marketing to internal customers, your team. In this chapter, we will discuss how to leverage digital marketing to keep your internal customers engaged and informed.

BUILDING YOUR DIGITAL STRATEGY

While many of the tools used to market to internal customers remain consistent with that of external customers, you need to approach this strategy from a different angle. Let us look at each step within the digital marketing strategy process from the perspective of the internal customer.

Step One: Know the Buyer

Before developing a marketing message, establish your Core Customer – in this case your staff.

I suggest creating an "internal customer avatar" for your typical employee, the same as you would for an external customer avatar. For a review of what a customer avatar is and how to develop one, please refer to Chapter four.

Step Two: What Is the Message?

When marketing to your external customers, it is important to ensure that you have a strong emphasis on gaining their attention – it is no different when marketing to your internal customers. It is true that your internal customers are already invested and therefore it can be argued that you already have their attention, however, in my experience this can be a misleading assumption. Although you already may have the invested attention of most of your internal customers, I would argue that to keep their engagement requires a strong emphasis on gaining their attention consistently. In addition to gaining their attention, you need to consider the value that you are creating for your internal customer and the way you are presenting your content. Finally, the same as marketing to external customers, you need to be clear on the purpose of your internal marketing and the next steps or action that you want your employees to take as a result of consuming your content. Remember, every message needs to have a purpose and reason for doing it; otherwise it is simply a waste of time for everyone involved.

Consider this – how are you adding an element of entertainment to your content to keep your internal customer engaged in the message and looking forward to the next internal email blast or video message?

Step Three: The Vehicle

When marketing to your internal customers, it is important to consider which tools you will be utilizing to deliver the message. There is not one right way to deliver content – it depends on the audience.

For example, one company that we consulted with has over 4,000 employee truck drivers. These employees are busy and are on the road constantly with little time to sit down and read a company newsletter or even watch a corporate video message. Knowing this, the company took their internal newsletter and created a podcast specifically to serve their employee truck drivers – creating ease of access when digesting content while their people are actively driving.

On the other hand, before he sold his company, CEO and Founder Ron Lovett of Source Security, led an organization of over 500 employees – primarily security guards – throughout Canada. To streamline communication, Ron turned to video as his vehicle to transmit information, company updates and security tips, and using humor to keep the content entertaining and engaging. Doing this, he knew that employees would always look forward to watching the next video.

SHOOT FOR THE STARS

While open rates in the 5-10% range can be considered substantial when marketing to external customers, for internal customers, your approach must be to aim for a 100% consumption rate and settle for no less than 95%. Your employees are your brand champions and keeping them engaged and well-informed is not only good business, but will help them feel appreciated in the workplace. Therefore, when communicating to internal customers, you must ensure that three criteria are always met:

1. **Deliver value.** This is obvious, but make sure your communication is relevant and useful. Don't communicate for the sake of communicating. Have a purpose and value to deliver.
2. **Be entertaining and engaging.** You want your employees to gain value, yes, however, you also want them to enjoy the experience and look forward to the next message from your company.
3. **Provide content in various mediums.** Not everyone consumes content in

the same way. For some, they may prefer reading the company newsletter, while for others it needs to be a video, email communication or perhaps a podcast. For this reason, I strongly suggest that you distribute your content in three formats: Read It (articles/listicles), Watch It (videos) and Listen to It (podcasts/free recorded messages). Make it easy to achieve your 100% consumption rate!

In the 90s and early 2000s, it was believed that the most important person within a company was the CEO and the second most important person was the CFO. Shortly after, Silicon Valley's war on talent pushed the head of HR to the top. But today, one of the most important strategies that determine a company's success lies in its marketing. Marketing to both internal and external customers. Are you leveraging your marketing?

Chapter Eight

Trends in Digital Marketing and Strategies to Stay Current

"I believe you have to be willing to be misunderstood if you're going to innovate."
– Jeff Bezos

THE EVOLUTION OF GREEN VILLAGE HOME & GARDEN'S CONTENT STRATEGY

In the early 90s when distributing a newsletter was as cutting-edge as the term "social media," my team at *Green Village Home & Garden* developed and sent out our first newsletter. It was two colors, printed on white paper, eight pages long, and the headline read, "Welcome to the inaugural issue of the *Green Village Garden Guide*." Our content covered tips on how to select the right type of flowers for backyards, community events and news on charity organization we supported.

Our experiment of sending out a newsletter was such a success, that I still remember manually entering the first few hundred names of subscribers and addresses into a database. People loved receiving the personal education-based content that we provided each quarter, and they loved hearing from us.

The newsletter eventually grew to 32,000 names. Even though production costs increased drastically to nearly $15,000 per issue, it was worth the investment. Our eight-page *Green Village Garden Guide* was repeatedly voted the most effective marketing that we did in our annual customer marketing survey.

By the year 2000, our buyer was becoming more tech savvy – everyone had email addresses, which opened an opportunity for us to distribute a shorter monthly newsletter through email. While it was slow to catch on, we eventually grew our email database to 20,000 active readers – which benefited us as production costs were low relative to our quarterly newsletters, and we were able to connect with our buyers more frequently. Because of its deep connection and effectiveness, we continued to send out the longer format eight-page newsletters every quarter, however, now we were able for the first time to increase our connection frequency with our clients by sending regular short format email newsletters every month.

Even though the vehicle of communication of a printed newsletter versus an email newsletter evolved, the content remained consistent. Content remained king and education-based content that was personalized for our area and buyer was a huge win for us.

In late 2007, Facebook had reached its first 100,000 business pages. Similar to email, the vehicle for delivering content and the frequency that content was delivered had changed, but the message itself essentially remained consistent. Over time, we added YouTube, Twitter and other social media tools to our marketing arsenal and repertoire.

While the vehicle for delivering content has evolved – and continues to do so – providing education-based content will always remain key for a successful digital marketing strategy. As technology and methods of consumption continue to change, remember that it is crucial to stay up-to-date on trends.

TIPS FOR STAYING ON TREND

The frequency of change is accelerating, and the idea of staying on trend can be overwhelming. To help keep pace, consider these two tips:

1. Look to thought leaders – Pay attention to marketing thought leaders; after all, they have built a name on knowing what is hot and what is about to be. Some of my favorite thought leaders today including Jay Baer, bestselling author of *Youtiliy,* Joe Polish, President of Piranha Marketing Inc. and Creator of Genius Network, Dean Graziosi, author of *Millionaire Success Habits*, Seth Godin, marketing guru and author of many books including *Purple Cow*, and David Meerman Scott, author of *Real Time Marketing & PR.*

2. Asking your customers should be a regular habit – Ask your customers

where they get their content and how they prefer it delivered. By asking questions, you can receive great information on your customer's content consumption and buying habits. For example, the first time I heard about Facebook was actually from a customer – that insight eventually inspired me to utilize Facebook for our business.

TRENDS TO WATCH

What makes trends so exhilarating is that they are constantly changing. The trends I write about today may be completely different from the ones I'd discuss by the time this book is published. It is important to be mindful that trends are constantly changing. However, it would be worth your while to keep the below identified trends as inspiration for further research:

1. **Podcasting** – Due to the ease of consumption – listening while driving, jogging or cleaning the house – podcasting has become increasingly prevalent to consumers. In a 2017 Edison Research report, it was identified that 24% of Americans ages 12 and up have listened to a podcast in the past month, which is the same number of Americans on Twitter.

2. **Over-The-Top Advertising (OTT)** – OTT refers to video ads on streaming services like YouTube or Hulu. According to Lauren Davenport, CEO of the Symphony Agency, "With a growing number of US households using some type of streaming service, there is great potential, because the platforms that offer advertising often require the user to watch the full ad before programming will resume." Say goodbye to channel surfing!

3. **Influencer Marketing** – Influencer marketing taps the thought leaders in your industry as brand advocates. Influencers in your industry carry a lot of weight and in some cases, they carry more weight than big industry players. For example, in the beauty and fashion industry, "86% of the most-viewed beauty videos on YouTube were made by influencers, compared to 14% of beauty brands." And, "57% of beauty and fashion companies use influencers as part of their marketing strategies."

4. **Virtual Reality and 360 Video** – Increasingly, companies are tapping virtual reality and 360 videos to show off products to consumers using Google Cardboard, among other VR devices. For example, Volvo released a virtual reality test drive for the launch of their XC90 SUV. The VR test drive resulted in 175,000+ views on YouTube and 155 reviews on Google Play. It was also a great tour for consumers that were not located near a Volvo dealership. Etihad Airlines tapped VR using Google Cardboard to show consumers the unique experience of flying in one of their Airbus A380 planes including a tour of the

economy class, first class and even "the residence," which features a three-room cabin with a butler.

5. **Augmented Reality** – Through technology, there are many ways to bring together traditional print marketing with online marketing through augmented reality. Your company's magazine ad can now come to life on the screen of your cell phone when scanned using an augmented reality app. Suddenly, the car you are featuring in the print ad, comes to life in a video and starts driving that person through a test course.

6. **Chatbots** – A chatbot (Chat Robot) is a computer program that "maintains a conversation with a user in natural language, understands the intent of the user and sends a response based on business rules and data of the organization." Small to large businesses are incorporating chatbot technology on their websites, Facebook Messenger and more to provide personalized responses to customer's questions. According to a Business Intelligence report, "Investments in the chatbot industry grew 229% between 2015 and 2016."

BE BRAVE AND EXPERIMENT

When I am speaking with entrepreneurs and marketers, I continually run across one big problem – the fear of experimentation and what can go wrong. I would rather you experiment with six different tools and keep two of them than suffer from analysis paralysis and find yourself behind the eight ball. Be brave and experiment with new tools. It will be well worth it for you and your brand!

Chapter Nine

How Print Marketing Adds Credibility and Longevity

"Content is King." – Bill Gates

Almost 125 years ago, the first company-branded magazine was published and is still in circulation today. John Deere's *The Furrow* was first published in 1885 – a magazine that combined advertising of John Deere products with agricultural tips.

Circulation grew, and in 1912 their reach was over 4 million consumers.

That same year, John Deere purchased their first electric printing press for printing the magazine, "spending what amounts to $850,000 in 2013 on a press that printed in two colors and spat out 50,000 issues in eight hours."

Today, the magazine is circulated to 2 million consumers globally with 80% of consumers still preferring paper to electronic – regardless of the demographic.

"I've never worked for a brand magazine like this that people loved so much," explains publication manager David Jones. "Telling stories that folks enjoy reading – and that they can use in their own operations – has been the recipe since the beginning."

Before there were podcasts, videos and blogs, there was print, the original method to document and distribute a message. Still today, print is considered more credible than anything found online.

Content, the oldest form of communication, has gone through an interesting evolution. Starting in 2000 BC, Ancient Egyptians first utilized content by carving on steel and papyrus to distribute public notices. Sears essentially invented direct marketing when they sent out 8,000 postcards in 1882 and received 2,000 orders in return.

Almost a century later in 1994, the pioneering push into digital marketing was made with the very first online banner ad, created on hotwired.com for Volvo, AT&T and Spirit, among other name brands.

As the creation and distribution of content grows, so does the sheer amount of available information – including good and bad content. For example, consider the article "Anywhere the Eye Can See, It's Likely to See an Ad" from the *New York Times*: "Yankelovich, a market research firm, estimates that a person living in a city 30 years ago saw up to 2,000 ad messages a day, compared with up to 5,000 today."

When it comes to the quality of content, print has a higher perceived credibility than digital. For instance, if you read an advertising piece on a Facebook post, you may automatically discount it. But if you were presented with the same ad printed in Forbes magazine, you may feel differently and be more engaged.

Print has a longer longevity than digital, as most consumers are not going to throw away a book or magazine. Instead, they dog-ear favorite sections, underline and highlight the key takeaways and often pass it along to someone they know.

DOES PRINT PERFORM BETTER THAN DIGITAL?

According to a study by Temple University researchers, there are significant benefits to using print advertising. During the study, the researchers "used a variety of neuromarketing methods, including eye tracking and biometric measurements to gauge the initial reactions." One week later, the subjects were put in fMRI machines to "evaluate the longer-term impact of the ads."

The results – "subjects showed greater emotional response and memory for physical media ads. It also caused more activity in brain areas associated with value and desire."

In an additional study, researchers Alshaali and Varshney showed that consumers are more engaged when reading print material as opposed to digital, which is often skimmed. The study found that people "read digital screen text 20 to 30% slower than printed paper."

REACHING C-SUITE EXECUTIVES TAKES PRINT

Forbes Insights and Deloitte Center for Industry Insights surveyed "nearly 300 C-level executives to analyze how top executives prefer to receive business insights." According to their report, print plays a crucial role in providing information to C-level executives. In fact, "50% of C-suite says that reading business insights in print is still critical, particularly for longer pieces, and over 84% indicate that they would choose to read a four- to five-page report offline."

PUBLISHERS ARE THE FUTURE OF MARKETING?

In 1996, Bill Gates said, "Content is King." That statement continues to be true today, and increasingly grows in importance. In that same Forbes Insights and Deloitte Center for Industry Insights survey, CMOs were interviewed regarding the importance of content creation. According to the study, "Over 90% of CMOs agree that their organizations must develop a publishing function to execute their growth agenda and manage the rising cost and complexity of content operations."

Content is king – and tomorrow's marketers are publishers, and the easiest way to reach C-level executives is print marketing.

IT TAKES ALL THREE PILLARS TO MASTER THE BUYING CYCLE

While print is still considered more credible than digital, it is important to utilize all three pillars to cater to the needs of your ideal customer and guide them through the buying cycle. By creating content using each pillar, you are not only keeping the message alive in multiple ways, but you are attracting buyers that prefer different methods of communication.

Chapter Ten

It's More Affordable Than Ever to Utilize Print

_____

"Innovation is the only way to win!" – Steve Jobs

In 1965, Gordon Moore, co-founder of Intel, stated, "Computing technology will double every two years…making our computers faster and better by 100% every two years." Making history, Moore's Law is now used not only to describe the rate of advancement from computing technology, which is still accepted today, but is also a figurative description for innovation – regardless of the product or service.

While computing technology has been disrupted by fast innovation, so has print. Ten to fifteen years ago when trying to publish a book, you would have to move through many initial steps – first, you would have to convince a major publishing house to invest in your idea, and then the publisher would print huge quantities and invest in marketing the book. Most publishing houses put that time and money behind big stars as opposed to diversifying their portfolio with lesser-known authors.

Thanks to innovation, printing today is more affordable and accessible to utilize than ever before. Authors now have a plethora of options to self-publish as opposed to going to large publishing houses. For example, many printing houses now provide the ability to print books in small batches of 1,000 or less. Amazon allows anyone to upload an ebook, and the work to assemble your book can be freelanced at a fraction of the cost.

In fact, authors do not even have to print batches at all. In 2015, Amazon purchased

CreateSpace.com, a printing company that specializes in on-demand print. In other words, instead of doing minimum print runs in the thousands, CreateSpace.com prints a single copy of a book each time certain books are purchased on the Amazon platform.

With the help of the self-publishing movement, more and more people are now able to position themselves as the thought leaders in their industry by publishing a book. In fact, according to Bowker Report, "727,000 U.S. Self-Published ISBNs were created in 2015. That's a 21% increase from 2014 to 2015."

Similar to the book publishing industry, magazines also underwent a major revolution. Today, anyone can create their own branded magazine without large capital or time investments. This is where Carle Publishing has found a real niche in the industry.

Leading the charge, Carle Publishing is guiding organizations and thought leaders through the magazine production process of creating content strategies, providing ghost writers, collaborating with big name celebrities and authors, designing the look and feel of the magazine and handling distribution logistics.

Services like this did not exist five years ago.

When I was running *Green Village Home & Garden,* we issued a two-color, eight-page quarterly newsletter for 20 years. The newsletter was an effective tool that enabled us to own the ink in our space, however, it was expensive. When we finally made the transition from newsletters to magazines, we were able to do it at a fraction of the cost. Instead of publishing an eight-page, two-color newsletter, firms now print and distribute 32-page full-color magazines. The cost is substantially lower because Carle Publishing takes advantage of massive economies of scale in the production process and printing – and the Client-Partners Carle Publishing works with can supplement part of the investment in their magazine by selling advertising sponsorship space.

How do you get started? It is simple.

Publish a magazine by doing it yourself, or by using a publishing house, like Carle Publishing.

Whether you do it yourself or use the services of a publisher, below are some of my recommended steps to get started.

STEP ONE – CONTENT STRATEGY

When creating a content strategy, you must first consider the audience you are targeting. Go back to your notes on your Core Customer and consider whom you are really trying to reach, what topics they would find interesting and valuable and how you can use your value-added content to influence their buying decision. When choosing the topics, you want to be sure that they are valuable, worth reading and cause the audience to take some kind of action. However, you also want to make sure that your magazine articles have some entertainment value in the graphic design and layout, so that your Core Customer not only gains value by reading your content, but that they look forward to receiving your next issue. It is crucial to not just have great content, but to also present your content in an entertaining way with the right formatting, flow and layout.

STEP TWO – COORDINATE THE CONTENT

Now that you have your content strategy in place, unless you want to tackle all aspects of your magazine, I suggest that you gather your freelance ghostwriters, guest contributors – if you choose to include them – editors and graphic designers. Ensure that your writer does not double as your editor and that your graphic designer has an eye for details.

STEP THREE – GATHER ADVERTISING

Cut down on production and distribution costs while simultaneously building legitimacy and selling advertising sponsorships in your magazine.

I would recommend creating a media kit to demo your magazine to potential advertisers. When considering who you should approach, start with your vendors and suppliers. I'm a believer in starting with companies who you do business with, and those who will benefit from your sales growth.

STEP FOUR – PRINT

When it comes to printing your magazine, consider your local newspaper or commercial printer, or simply shop online for a printer. Be sure that you understand the appropriate specs and sizes for your magazine before you go – pricing can vary immensely depending on paper size and quality.

If you decide to go with a printing company, they can guide you on the most economical way to create and structure your magazine for print. Keep in mind, like all types of printing, your first magazine off the press will cost you a small fortune in time and money – and any additional copies will cost only pennies. Do not be surprised if printing 10,000 copies of your magazine costs little more than printing 1,000 copies as the content, layout and physical printing setup is already done. After printing your first copy, costs associated with additional copies consist primarily of paper and ink.

STEP FIVE – DISTRIBUTION

You will want to save several copies of your printed magazine for yourself to hand out at your place of business, trade shows, etc. You will then want to send a copy to current clients to keep them engaged. Finally, you may want to utilize the remaining magazines – the bulk of your production – for prospective customers. You can purchase a mailing list segmented by industry, geography, business size, household size, gender, income and more. Once purchased, utilize your printing house or a fulfillment house to prepare and address your magazines. Working with the post office, you can work through the paperwork and coordinate your distribution logistics and costs.

WANT TO DIY? CONSIDER THE COSTS ASSOCIATED WITH DIY MAGAZINE PUBLISHING

If you have the time to invest, then you can definitely DIY (do it yourself) your own magazine. Even when utilizing freelance work, you will want to budget 40 to 50 hours of your time to assemble a 32-page magazine. In addition to time, you should consider costs associated with printing and mailing magazines. While cost differs, you can expect to make an investment of $15,000 to $17,000 or more to write, produce, design, print and distribute 5,000 magazines.

YOU DON'T HAVE TO DIY

At our company, Carle Publishing, our goal is to make publishing a magazine as easy, effective and economical as possible. We take care of all the aforementioned steps, including:
- Identifying your target audience
- Creating a content strategy
- Writing your content (ghostwriting)

- Coordinating industry-leading guest contributors
- Designing your magazine
- Proofreading and editing
- Managing all printing production and logistics
- Creating an online version of the magazine for iPads and eReaders, social media, websites, etc.
- And all distribution logistics including targeted list purchasing, labeling and postal costs

All of the above can be provided for a flat rate, which is often 30-40% cheaper than DIY methods.

Instead of investing 40 hours to create a magazine, Carle Publishing breaks it down into tasks that can take 4 hours for Client-Partners. In fact, we have Client-Partners who have literally turned their magazines around in under 2 hours. Because of our efficient production process and the millions of magazines we print each year for Client-Partners, you can take advantage of our economies of scale in the production cost of the magazine to printing and even postal distribution.

To help you secure advertising sponsors, we create an ad sponsorship toolkit, which includes a customized media kit, video, email template and more. Using our toolkit, on average Client-Partners subsidize 70-80% of their investment.

Further, when Client-Partners leverage a semi-customized model, a portion of the magazine is dedicated to nationally renowned thought leaders as guest writers. The thought leaders are chosen specifically for your target audience so content is not only of interest to your readers, but it also boosts the credibility of your magazine.

Chapter Eleven

From Advertiser to Advisor – How Print Publishing Provides a Leg Up on the Competition

---

"Think of yourself as a resource to your clients; an advisor, counselor, mentor and friend." – Brian Tracy

When Verne Harnish, Growth Guru and founder of the Entrepreneur's Organization, instructed my MIT Birthing of Giants class to "Own the Ink in Your Industry," he was encouraging us to become thought leaders by publishing our own material. For Verne, it did not matter if that entrepreneur owned a retail garden center, or the hottest tech startup – according to Verne, "Whatever your customers are reading, you should have it come from you." The action of publishing your own book or magazine places you in a position of authority, enabling you to create instant credibility and gain an unfair advantage over the competition.

Consider your competition – each and every one of them is conducting some form of print advertising, newspaper, magazine ads, brochures, white papers, etc. That is because in order to be present in the marketplace, they need to have a print advertising strategy to complement their other forms of marketing, even if it is a simple brochure featuring their products or services.

Of those competitors, let us consider that maybe 10% take their print marketing strategy to the next level by contributing value-added content in the local newspaper or trade magazine. As a contributing author, they can start to make the transition from advertiser to advisor – and effectively own a portion of the buyers' mindshare.

A friend of mine owns the largest car dealership in our region – and part of his content strategy is writing a column called "Ask the Experts" for the local newspaper. This column provides information on cars and car buying to potential customers. While he pays the newspaper for access to that column, the content he delivers is valuable to readers. He states that, "It's worth it for me, even if I have to pay for it, to have someone else acknowledge me as an expert."

If your competition is conducting print advertising, and 10% take it to the next level by contributing content in someone else's publication, then think of the impact you can have by creating your own publication – which could be a book or a magazine. Using this strategy allows you to dominate your industry by providing educational content that builds trust and credibility. After all, you can then position yourself and your brand to be more than a published contributor; you actually "own the ink in your industry" – becoming the top 1% authority figure in your marketplace.

GET JACK'D! – JACK DALY'S BRANDED MAGAZINE DIFFERENTIATES HIS IMAGE FROM THE COMPETITION

"Issuing a magazine is like distributing a mini book every six months!" states Jack Daly, sales guru and 12-time published author. For Jack, his magazine entitled *Get Jack'd!* is a huge benefit because it allows him to publish his newest ideas on paper and despite the fact that Jack has published over 12 books, "something like 90% of competing sales consultants also write books; creating a magazine is unique to me, and people like that."

HOW TO ENHANCE CREDIBILITY ASSOCIATED WITH YOUR BRANDED MAGAZINE

In addition to writing educational content, you can enhance the credibility of your branded magazine by introducing guest writers and advertisers. When big-name guest writers appear in your publication, it sends a strong message to readers that others believe in your magazine and want to be a part of it. Inviting them to contribute content is a win for everyone involved. Your audience is provided great content by thought leaders in their space, your big-name contributors get free exposure and your publication gains credibility that contributors bring by having their name associated with your magazine.

Advertisements inside a magazine are just as important. A magazine without some form of advertising may be looked upon as a glorified newsletter. However, when you include some advertisers, it shows that your magazine has enough value that others will pay to be included. As such, advertising inside a magazine provides two benefits: a revenue source to offset some of your investment and, just as importantly, it provides additional credibility.

THERE ARE INTERNAL BENEFITS TO PUBLISHING A MAGAZINE

Like the prize inside a Cracker Jack box, we have seen an unexpected benefit to publishing custom branded magazines – employee pride and recruiting. It is not unusual for our Client-Partners to share that their employees love the magazine as much as, if not more than, the owners or decision-makers do.

When we started Carle Publishing in 2012, one of the early pieces of feedback we received was that it increased the pride employees felt for their company and the magazine functioned as a differentiator when recruiting top talent.

One of Carle Publishing's Client-Partners stated that his branded magazine not only gave him credibility and status among his existing clients and potential customers, but that it also gave his company strong brand positioning among people within his industry. According to that Client-Partner, his magazine allowed him to "hire four of the best salespeople away from the competition." Although he could not say that it was the primary reason, he did confirm that the magazine was brought up in each and every interview by the prospective new salespeople. "They were all very impressed by the level of professionalism we put out into the marketplace through our magazine."

Chapter Twelve

Develop Effective Personal Interactions Through a Complete Marketing Strategy

"Connecting with others is rewarding; it makes us feel like we aren't alone in the world" – Jonah Berger

During my 20 years as a retailer at *Green Village Home & Garden,* we took pride on being excellent marketers – we utilized elements of both print and digital to attract buyers to our retail locations. However, when a buyer came to our store, it was only considered a sale after they made the actual purchase at the cash register, which regularly came after speaking with a customer service representative (CSR).

At the end of the day, it did not matter how effective our digital and print marketing was to reel a new prospect into our store; in most cases, speaking with a CSR needed to happen before a sale was made.

The third pillar of marketing – interactive marketing – is when a prospect interacts in an actual conversation with a member of your company. It includes face-to-face conversations, presentations, events, webinars, phone calls and even chat functions.

IT TAKES ALL THREE MARKETING PILLARS TO MAKE A SALE

In Chapter Four, we learned that before a buyer is willing to make a purchase, they need to interact with a company an average of eight times. For 95% of products and services, a buyer is not going to make a purchase after seeing a single advertisement

– to make a sale, they have to be led through the buying cycle through the use of the three pillars.

When you are utilizing print and digital marketing, often engagement from the buyer is limited since you are most often having a one-way conversation – you dish out material and the buyer consumes it.

Not so when it comes to interactive marketing – instead, you interact in real-time with a prospect in actual conversation.

Interactive marketing is essentially content marketing on a more personal level, whether it be one-on-one, at an event or presentation.

This is often the last step in the buying cycle, as many buyers need to interact with the company to validate that they are selecting the product or service that best fits their needs.

LOOKING AT SALES THROUGH A MARKETING LENS

Often, Client-Partners tell us, "We do some marketing, but for us, to grow our revenues, it really comes down to my salespeople's ability to find a lead and make a sale." However, the first interaction a salesperson has with a prospect is marketing, not a sales conversation.

First interactions are crucial. A salesperson's job is to spread the word about their product or service and attract the lead into the buying cycle, which is a marketing function. This means that their initial conversation with a prospect is drastically different from their closing conversation.

Consider SalesForce.com and their sales process. They have a large number of salespeople on staff throughout their various call centers. From the outside, you could easily assume that everyone on their sales teams performs similar functions. However, when you uncover their sales process, you find something quite different. Their sales teams are broken down into two primary functions: lead generation and sales.

Lead generators perform a different function than the sales teams. In fact, lead generators fall under a different department, as their job is to make discovery calls to attract leads and make appointments for the sales team. This is purely a marketing function and, for most companies, is part of the marketing strategy and budget. For lead generator teams, once a lead is identified and turned into a sales opportunity, meaning the prospect agrees to a discovery phone call, that contact is passed into the sales teams' hands to close.

When you break down any sales process, the first interaction should be a marketing function – your interactive marketing pillar. To align with the interactive marketing pillar, it is imperative that you think through your messaging, your collateral and the way your company presents itself to that prospect so that it is consistent with your digital and print marketing messaging.

Let us say that you have attracted a prospect through the early stages of your buying cycle by leveraging clear and concise messaging in your digital and print marketing. However, when they first make contact with a salesperson or customer service representative, the messaging is inconsistent or different altogether. What happens to their trust in your company and brand?

Now contrast that to a customer's buying experience where your digital and print messaging is completely aligned with their first conversation they have with a salesperson – totally different experience. Their trust in your brand is much stronger, and that prospect is more apt to move all the way through the buying cycle and make a purchasing decision.

Your digital, print and interactive marketing must have the same concise messaging to instill brand trust.

THERE ARE ALWAYS EXCEPTIONS TO THE RULE

For over 90% of businesses, interactive marketing is an important and often required stage of the buying cycle, though there are always exceptions to the rule. For example, Amazon does not need interactive marketing to close a sale.

Amazons of the world excluded, interactive marketing is a crucial component to the buying cycle and actually closing deals. And you better make certain that the initial in-person messaging is aligned with your first two pillars of marketing.

Chapter Thirteen

Leveraging Presentations and Events to Solidify Your Status as a Thought Leader

---

"A talk is a voyage with a purpose, and it must be charted. The man who starts out going nowhere, generally gets there." – Dale Carnegie

"In the last year alone, I have spoken at an average of four to five industry conferences, universities, and start-up accelerator events per month," explains WelkerMedia CEO Artem Welker in his blog post.

WelkerMedia is a nonprofit media organization that empowers creatives, civic creators and changemakers across the world through their award-winning school and acceleration program among other services.

According to Welker, he leverages presentations as a highly effective platform to rope in leads. "I only charge for about 50% of my speaking sessions because they help me generate so much revenue."

Why are presentations both an effective and efficient way to reel in prospects? A mentor once told me, "It's one thing to say you're an expert and another thing to have someone else recognize and highlight you as one." When providing a presentation at an event, the event organizer or sponsor validates you as an expert and pays you for your valued expertise.

Not only do presentations work as a sales tool because they highlight you as an industry expert, but you are able to leverage your time to influence dozens, hundreds or thousands of individuals at one time as opposed to talking with prospects one-on-one.

In this chapter, we will discuss how to create memorable presentations and the presentation pyramid.

HOW DO YOU CREATE A MEMORABLE PRESENTATION?

Have you ever attended an event and had a presenter resonate with you? No matter the length of their speech, five minutes or a two-hour keynote, when done right, a presentation is not easily forgotten and will often inspire you to take action.

To ensure that you deliver a presentation that is just as engaging, there are two tactics that you must consider:

1. **Honing your presentation skills**

   Whether you are conducting a webinar for 10 people, or keynoting a two-hour presentation before a much larger audience, your presentation must be polished and professional. Consider the one, two or three takeaways you want the audience to learn and deliver them in a clear and concise way.

   If you do not consider yourself a presenting aficionado, consider joining Toastmasters International. Toastmasters International is a non-profit organization that spans 142 countries with 15,900 clubs and is focused on developing your presentation skills.

   I joined Toastmasters after hearing Tom Peters, author on business management, speak at a conference almost 20 years ago. He gave a presentation that was so memorable that is still resonates with me today. During his talk, he strongly encouraged all business leaders to join the organization to strengthen their presentation and communication skills. I later learned that many other big names have been members of the organization, including Tim Allen (actor) and former US President Bill Clinton.

   Want to learn more about Toastmasters International? Visit: www. toastmasters.org.

2. **Providing visual aids**

   Memorable presentations use memorable visual aids or likewise, none at all.

Often, the most disengaging presentations are those read from a textbook of slides. Do not waste your audience's time with boring presentations – use few-to-no text in your slides, and instead incorporate pictures or graphics to tie an idea back to your presentation.

Two excellent resources to learn more about visual aids are *Presentation Zen* by Garr Reynolds and *The Presentation Secrets* of Steve Jobs by Carmine Gallo.

FOUR LEVELS OF PRESENTATIONS

There are four levels of presentations and as you become known as an authority and prove yourself an engaging speaker who delivers value, you will be able to work your way up the different levels of the pyramid.

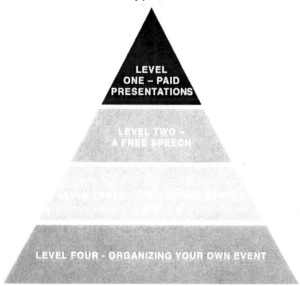

LEVEL 4 – ORGANIZING YOUR OWN EVENT

Organizing your own branded event is an excellent way to start doing presentations, as this will help you attract the audience you are looking for. If your company has developed enough of its brand to draw in your own audience, consider if it is cost effective to organize your own event to sell or resell to clients.

What is involved in organizing your own event? Here are four action items to consider:

1. Select a venue in a city where your business has a lot of contacts. The more contacts you have in a city, the easier it will be to draw in an audience.
2. Create the content and find any needed speakers. What will the theme of your event be? Do you need to secure any outside speakers for your event?
3. Set up your marketing campaign. Create your landing page for attendees to register and look to digital or print marketing tactics to help reel in an audience.
4. Create a follow-up strategy for after the event. How will you stay in touch with your audience? Did you give them a next step to learn more about your products/service/message?
5. What's your return on investment? Keep track of costs associated with the event and any revenue incurred because of the event.

HOLGANIX FORGOES EXPENSIVE TRADESHOWS IN FAVOR OF EVENTS

Traditionally, Holganix, a manufacturer of plant probiotics that allows contractors and farmers to reduce the amount of chemicals needed to nurture healthy plants, attended trade shows like most green industry companies to reel in leads. Their ROI was not easily traced and the CEO, Barrett Ersek, was wondering if he was creating excitement – not deals.

In 2017, Holganix stopped purchasing booth spaces at 90% of their trade shows and instead allocated the expenses to creating regional events called Bionutritional Summits in partnership with local distributors.

During their 2017 tour, they held 16 regional *Bionutritional Summits* and touched 390 customers or prospects, providing a forecasted $600,000 in annual revenue. Holganix also reports spending 60% less on their regional events as compared to purchasing booth space at trade shows. The contractors are engaged at the event, not just because Holganix solves their agronomic and environmental problems but because the speakers are highly credentialed and provide content in a memorable and entertaining way.

Regardless of which level or strategy you use for your presentations, your presentation content must be memorable and valuable. If you get on stage and bomb, it will not only hurt the event; it will hurt your chances of being invited to do more presentations and most damaging, it will hurt your brand.

LEVEL 3 – SPONSORING EVENTS

Another way to get in front of an audience is to sponsor a tradeshow or event to gain a speaking slot. This strategy works quite well, and I do recommend it when you are first starting out, or when it is the only way to get in front of a target audience.

MY PERSONAL PRESENTATION STRATEGY THAT DELIVERS VALUE AND PROMOTES MY BUSINESS

When I was in retail, we often went to home shows with the understanding that we would pay for the largest booth, and in return, be given an exclusive opportunity to speak and demonstrate our products, shutting our competition out as a presenter at the same show.

Today, I speak dozens of times each year to audiences about Influencer Marketing, Internal Marketing and of course The Three Pillars of Marketing. The presentations are professionally choreographed, and the messaging is extremely valuable.

I am asked to do a number of paid keynotes each year, which is preferred, and when the audience is right, I always accept the invitation. For the right audience, meaning our target audience, we occasionally offer to do free presentations, with paid expenses only. This provides value and helps us gain exposure.

When an opportunity arises for us to be in front of a target audience that we feel we absolutely need to be in front of, we will also consider sponsoring the event to acquire a small presentation slot. However, like the Holganix story (above), we no longer attend trade shows or events without first confirming a speaking engagement or presentation opportunity.

Side Note #1: Does it work? For us, it does. Over the past few years, we have seen our return on presentations be anywhere from $50,000 to $400,000 of new annualized business – and event organizers continually ask for us to return. Which in my mind, is a success.

Side Note #2: Depending on your product or service, you may be able to barter services for sponsorship. For certain events, Carle Publishing will do this by providing a fully customized magazine for the event in exchange for sponsorship and time on stage. It is an opportunity to be a win-win for both parties.

LEVEL 2 – A FREE SPEECH

Providing a free speech is an excellent way to get started and solve a problem for event organizers. This provides them with great content without compromising their budget. Even free speeches can be difficult gigs to land, as there are so many others who want to be known for their expertise. The way to get there is by perfecting your messaging and presenting speeches that are truly memorable. You can never "wing it" or provide subpar content. Each presentation is an opportunity to win business and work your way up the speaking pyramid – you cannot afford to waste any of it.

JACK DALY USES PRESENTATIONS AND EVENTS TO BUILD A BUSINESS AND A CAREER

When I first met Jack Daly, he was running a mortgage business and was looking to grow. To do so, he began providing free speeches at industry events, which raised the status and perception of his mortgage company. As time went on, Jack moved up the speaking pyramid and began to get paid to keynote industry events.

When he sold his business, he fell into public speaking professionally. He is now a highly paid public speaker due to the value he provides through his memorable, high-energy and entertaining presentations.

To further grow his brand, Jack has coupled his public speaking with print and digital marketing. He is a published author, which includes several books as well as his own branded magazine. Additionally, his social media following is exceptional.

LEVEL 1 – PAID PRESENTATIONS

Many in the business world aspire to be at the level where they are getting paid to present on a topic or keynote an event. When you start charging for events, you may notice that your demand actually starts to grow. The reason for this is because for many event organizers, identifying good speakers over exceptional speakers, price is often looked to as an indicator of value.

To reach level 1, and get paid to speak, you will need to hire:
1. A speech coach
2. A presentation consultant to help create the presentation slides
3. A freelance videographer or firm to create a demo reel – a professionally produced promotional video to get you hired

Chapter Fourteen

Getting to the Purchasing Decision

"In order to be irreplaceable, one must always be different." – Coco Chanel

When shuffling through your mail in the morning, you stumble across a Best Buy piece with an irrefutable offer.

Later that day, when scrolling through your Facebook feed, you notice an advertisement with that same offer. Intrigued, you swing by your local Best Buy on your way back from work and are greeted by a sales associate on the floor whose message mirrors the same offer you saw in the mail and on social media.

Best Buy is a firm that has truly nailed consistency across the three pillars of marketing.

To ensure your chances for successful interactive marketing, your face-to-face messaging must remain consistent with all digital and print interactions. Any inconsistencies in messaging will negatively impact the buying experience.

The next time you walk into a Best Buy, pay attention to their pitch, and ask yourself, how does it compare to their print and digital marketing? If they have a good sales manager in the store who trains their associates correctly, you will find it to be very consistent.

Andrew Davis, a professional speaker on branding, is an advocate for consistent messaging across all aspects of a firm's brand. From the business card, the website, to the actual appearance of a firm's CEO, every touch point must remain consistent for the buyer. For example, as a professional speaker, he advocates that it is crucial that your headshot remain consistent throughout all material, including the website, book, and your actual "look" during your presentation.

If you have a beard in your headshot on your website and book and you show up to do a presentation clean shaven, then you damage your consistency and subconsciously, the trust in the audience's mind.

Seth Godin, marketing guru, prides himself on his *remarkable* look, which sets him apart from other speakers. His look – yellow glasses, bald head and quizzical expression – is the same on his social media outlets, the inside cover of his latest book and when giving a presentation.

Consistency is everything.

IS YOUR MESSAGING CONSISTENT?

Are there inconsistencies between your print and digital marketing, and how your sales team explains your brand? Does your email use the same wording as your latest PowerPoint presentation? Do you have a clear and concise 30-second elevator pitch that appears in your digital and print marketing, and that your sales associates recite in the exact same way?

Hopefully, the answer to the above is that they are consistent. But for most of us, our messaging is not as consistent as we think.

Here are three tactics to ensure you have consistency throughout every aspect of your business:

1. SCRIPTS

I am a huge proponent of scripts to guide salespeople in their messaging, however, I do not believe they should be read verbatim.

Scripts are not to be repeated word for word; instead they should be well-organized, bulleted lists of the key takeaways. This is the language a salesperson should use when speaking to a buyer.

While scripts should not be repeated word for word, the sales team should have the opportunity to weigh in, without changing key vocabulary, to ensure that flow and formatting represent their selling approach.

Make sure to be comfortable, but also be consistent.

2. TRAINING

Remember the Earl Nightingale quote from Chapter Two?

"Reading one hour per day in your chosen field will make you an international expert in seven years."

Sales training is not just one part of the onboarding process for your organization; it should remain a staple goal throughout your sales team's employment.

That being said, it is important for your sales personnel to out-read and out-learn all competition. Consider doing two hours of sales training weekly – it will make the additional 38 hours of work more productive.

Through training, your ROI will be enormous. Trust me.

One of my favorite forms of training is *role practicing* – I stole this term from sales guru Jack Daly who made the distinction between role *playing* and role *practicing*. Just as NBA teams never practice during game times, neither should your team. NBA teams practice before they go onto the court to play a game. However, most sales organizations have their salespeople practice on real prospects.

Just like a coach makes his team practice relentlessly before the big game, so should your sales team be practicing *before* being placed in front of a potential buyer.

Make role *practicing* a key component of your sales training curriculum.

3. EVERYDAY COMMUNICATION

As the leader of your organization, if you want to have consistency in your messaging, it must start with you. One of the most basic requirements to achieving consistency is to lead by example and to use the appropriate vocabulary, which includes correcting your team when vocabulary is misused.

It takes all three pillars to make a sale, along with consistent messaging across all three pillars – especially during interactive marketing. If you are consistent in your marketing execution across all three pillars, it will put your buyer at ease, instill trust and enable their decision to buy much easier and your firm much more successful.

Get More Clients NOW

If YOU want to get attention and stand out visit www.CarlePublishing. com to learn more on how you can become a thought leader in digital & print marketing to compliment your interactive marketing!

Chapter Fifteen

Getting Started

Utilizing all three pillars to create a well-rounded and diverse marketing strategy.

"Focus on your strengths, not your weaknesses." – Gary Vaynerchuck

Is one marketing pillar more important than another?

Allure Medical Spa, a successful Detroit-based company, has multiple locations and focuses heavily on interactive marketing through presentations and events. Based on their activity, I would say they dedicate approximately 50% of their marketing resources to interactive marketing, 15% to print and 35% to digital.

Is Allure Medical Spa placing a higher level of importance on the interactive marketing pillar than the other pillars? Yes, they are! Ultimately, utilizing all three pillars is crucial when it comes to influencing your customer through the buying cycle and toward a purchasing decision – but depending on the products or services you provide, along with how your Core Customer prefers to consume content, one pillar may be weighed more or have a higher level of importance than another.

Allure Medical Spa owner Dr. Charles Mok, who enjoys interactive marketing, regularly conducts presentations in the Detroit area to not only generate leads, but to also heighten his credibility as a thought leader in the industry. Recording some of his speeches, he then turns them into videos on YouTube and shares them on his website as well as social media platforms like Facebook and Twitter.

And how does he utilize print? Through a branded magazine, published books and well-designed brochures to demonstrate the different procedures offered by the medical spa.

HOW SHOULD YOU WEIGH YOUR PILLARS?

Regardless of your industry and market, there are three key items to consider when deciding how to weigh your pillars – consider the product or service you're selling, understand your Core Customer and focus on your strengths.

1. **Your Products or Services** – Consider what it is you're selling. Are your products easily understood and explained? Do your services need more information or customization before a customer makes a buying decision? These are all questions to consider when determining the right mix for your company. For instance, if you are selling estate planning services, your customer will require a very high level of trust in you and your company before they make a purchasing decision. Therefore, your sales cycle will be heavily weighted toward interactive marketing. However, if you are selling an everyday product, perhaps digital and print marketing are going to be your heaviest weighted forms of marketing.

2. **Your Core Customer** – As stated in Chapter Four, your Core Customer is a fictional representation of the perfect buyer. You should know who they are, not only their demographics, but their likes, dislikes, habits and more. Consider how your buyer prefers to consume their content. It may sound simple, but the easiest way to discover how they prefer to receive their content is to ask them. As part of your customer onboarding process, ask them what had influenced their decision to purchase, how they first heard of you and what got them to officially become a customer.

3. **Your Strengths** – When in doubt, focus on your strengths, not your weaknesses. Which pillar do you excel at? If you excel at winning over audiences through your presentations, pour resources into getting more on-stage opportunities and spend time and money to improve your keynote content. Consider investing in high-quality graphics or a speech coach to help you script your presentation. Contemplate sponsoring an industry trade show and receive a speaking slot in return for your contribution. If you are talented and can connect to your audience online, do that. By pouring more resources into your strength, you can often reap higher rewards. When focusing on your strengths, regardless of what they may be, you can not only enjoy what you do, but be more effective.

COSTCO - FOCUSING ON THE EMPLOYEE TO BUILD SUPERIOR INTERACTIVE MARKETING

With over 700 locations representing the world's second largest retailer (second to Wal-Mart), Costco has a tendency to evenly use all three pillars, but favors interactive marketing. In my estimation, approximately 30% of their marketing resources are distributed to digital, 30% print and 40% interactive marketing.

Costco participates on social media, including their favorites, Facebook and Pinterest, and makes sure that when a buyer is searching for a product on Google, their ecommerce site is at or near the top of the page. They are also a huge fan of print and regularly dish out the *Costco Connection Magazine* to members in addition to their regular flyer programs. However, Costco is an organization that emphasizes the importance of face-to-face customer service by investing heavily in their employees to ensure that the interaction between employees and buyers exceeds expectations. In fact, the average hourly rate for an employee at Costco is 43% higher than the average hourly rate at Wal-Mart – proof that they really do invest in their people.

1-800-GOT-JUNK?

1-800-GOT-JUNK? Founder and CEO, Brian Scudamore, devotes a large portion of his marketing resources toward owning PR in both digital and print mediums. By doing so, his business has appeared on Hoarders, Property Brothers, Dr. Phil and even Oprah!

In addition to his hyper focus on PR opportunities, a second focus is on print through their street signs and recognizable trucks. In fact, Brian often encourages franchisees to lease an extra truck and park it, like a billboard, at a highly trafficked area. He dubs this practice "Parketing." According to Brian, it has a higher ROI than most other print advertising and doubles as a backup truck during periods of high demand.

Brian devotes the last portion of his marketing resources to interactive marketing. He relies on highly trained call center employees to convert inbound calls into actual sales for his franchise owners.

This combination has allowed Brian to build a business that does over $300 million annually for the franchise system. And, furthermore, his 1-800-GOT-JUNK? franchise is already sold out in nearly every city in the United States, Canada and Australia.

THE RIGHT MIX FOR YOU

If you want to dominate your industry and position your brand as the authority, you need to ask: what is the right marketing mix for my company? What is required to properly market my products or services? How do my Core Customers like to consume content? Where do my strengths lie?

To maximize your return on marketing dollars invested, you need to think strategically on how you want your expertise to be represented in the marketplace. Additionally, you need to identify which of the three pillars will most effectively influence your potential buyers. Is it digital marketing through social media? Is it print marketing through billboards or your own magazine? Or is it in interactive marketing through your front-line customer service people? Answering this question correctly will have a huge impact on your growth and prosperity long-term.

Chapter Sixteen

Easy Tactics to Get Started in Your Thought Leadership Journey

---

"People don't buy what you do; they buy why you do it." – Simon Sinek

You may be wondering, why do thousands of people stand in line for six hours to get the latest Apple product? According to Simon Sinek, it is because Apple understands their why. An advertisement from Apple does not read, "We make great computers. They're beautifully designed, simple to use and user-friendly. Wanna buy one?"

It is actually the opposite – through their advertising, Apple is essentially saying, "Everything we do, we believe in challenging the status quo. We believe in thinking differently. The way we challenge the status quo is by making our products beautifully designed, simple to use and user-friendly. We just happen to make great computers. Wanna buy one?"

In his TED *Talk How Great Leaders Inspire Action*, Simon states, "People don't buy what you do; they buy why you do it… the goal is not to do business with everyone who needs what you have; the goal is to do business with people that believe what you believe."

Yes – you understand the three pillars, and you know how to weigh each pillar to address your Core Customer, but, before you start digging into your first marketing tactic, consider your message. Instead of talking about *what* you sell and *how* your product or service is different, you should first identify *why* you do what you do.

Too often, I see organizations with incredible products that fail. Is it because their products are terrible? Is it because they did not use the right marketing pillars to get the word out? I would argue that it is often because they did not understand their why and therefore, could not communicate it effectively to their audience. There is disconnection between the story the company is telling and the story the buyer wants to hear. You may be selling a widget to a buyer, but that is not why your buyer purchases from you.

Remember Simon Sinek's statement, "People don't buy *what* you do; they buy *why* you do it."

THE ULTIMATE DRIVING EXPERIENCE – GROWING YOUR BUSINESS – OWNING THE INK

Yes, BMW sells high-quality, German cars (it is their what). And, yes, BMW creates that high-quality car by having the highest-quality leather interior and handling (it is their *how*), but their *why* is *to create the ultimate driving experience*. They do this by developing a better performing engine, providing the high-end handling technologies and the comfort of top-quality leather interiors. They just so happen to sell cars.

Benson Kearley IFG, sells commercial insurance to organizations. However, when you ask company President Steve Kearley, they do not see themselves as sellers of insurance; instead they are selling a business partnership. Instead of telling their prospects and clients about the latest insurance feature, the Benson Kearley IFG team spends a disproportionate amount of resources creating educational content on how to grow a business. They do this through business events featuring big-name speakers to educate their clients and prospects on businesses strategy and growth as well as through their *Risk & Business Magazine* that they publish and distribute to the local business community.

Kearley's clients do not purchase insurance because Benson Kearley IFG is cheaper or has a better service – they purchase because Benson Kearley IFG is a strategic partner and a resource to grow their business. Can you see the difference?

At Carle Publishing, our why is to *enable Client-Partners to Own the Ink in Their Industry, differentiating them in their industry or marketplace*. We accomplish the why through our custom branded magazine programs and digital marketing solutions. However, Client-Partners are not really purchasing a magazine program or online publishing platforms; they are buying the prestige and brand positioning that comes with publishing a customized magazine, videos or podcasts along with the convenience and ease of production. However, the real reason Client-Partners invest in branded magazines is because it provides enhanced brand positioning that ultimately leads to increased sales and market share.

Before you start tackling your three pillars, consider the reason behind why you do what you do. Why does your company exist? What is it that your customers are really buying from you? And as we've outlined in the above examples, it's not the products or services that you sell – it's something deeper.

>>Want to learn more about Simon Sinek? Check out his 18-minute TED Talk: https://www.ted.com/talks/simon_sinek_how_great_leaders_ inspire_action

LAST THOUGHTS ON OWNING THE INK

When I look back on everything we have discussed in the pages of this book, I am drawn back to the beginning – that singular moment while sitting at MIT's Birthing Of Giants class, when business guru Verne Harnish asked, "Whoever owns the ink in their industry is the one who creates instant credibility and gains an unfair advantage over their competition. Do you own the ink?"

If you want an unfair advantage over your competition, start with owning the ink. In other words, whatever your customers are reading or however they are educating themselves, have it come from you. The methodology to owning the ink is understanding how to utilize the three pillars, but before you even dig into the tactics around those pillars, understand that you are already an expert. If you have spent five-to-ten years or more in your given industry, you know something that 99.9% of society does not know. Acknowledge that you are a leader, harness the knowledge you already have, strengthen that knowledge through continual education and communicate that knowledge through the three pillars.

Understand who your Core Customer is, how they prefer to consume content and make a purchase. Ask your buyers where they go for information and be in that space. Is print more important to the buyer of your products or services? What about digital or interactive marketing? Which pillar is more important than the other and how are each of them weighed in level of importance to the buyer? When you go to craft a message, ask yourself if your story illustrates your *why* or purpose.

If you do not know how to get started – you are not alone. Owning the ink is an awesome concept and as a result figuring out which direction to take can be difficult.

I encourage you to look back at your notes and to consider what the one, two or three key takeaways are that you want to act on and implement in your business.

Stephen R. Covey, author of *The Seven Habits of Highly Effective People*, once stated, "Most of us spend too much time on what is urgent, and not enough time on what is important."

I have a personal habit of reading approximately two books per month; it allows me to think strategically about the business and to get out of the day-to-day grind.

Take advantage of the fact that reading a book forces you out of your daily routine and gets you to think strategically on what really matters to your business. Before picking up your next book or going about your daily business activity, consider setting aside some "strategic thinking" time at a coffee shop or at home, to outline your one, two or three takeaways and build a plan on how to implement those ideas into your business.

Once you have created an action plan, encourage your team to get involved. Ask them to read a section of the book that inspired that takeaway and walk them through your implementation plan.

Prioritize the important not the urgent.

Resources

Expand Your Knowledge

Looking to dig deeper into marketing, sales and strategy? Consider the below resources as a starting point to expand your knowledge. This is a list of my favorite marketing, sales and strategy-related business books and conferences.

Authors:
- *Scale Up* by Verne Harnish
- *The Average Joe* by Joe Polish
- *Hyper Sales Growth* by Jack Daly
- *Content Inc.* by Joe Pulizzi
- *Branding Is Sex* by Deb Gabor
- *The Ultimate Sales Machine* by Chet Holmes
- *The Challenger Sale* by Matthew Dickenson and Brent Adamson
- *Likeable Social Media* by Dave Kerpen
- *Story Selling* by Nick Nanson
- *Contagious:* Why Things Catch On by Jonah Berger
- *Blue Ocean Strategy* by W. Chan Kim
- *New Rules of Sales and Service* by David Meerman-Scott
- *To Sell Is Human* by Daniel Pink
- *Purple Cow* by Seth Godin
- *Jobs to Be Done* by Stephen Wunker, Jessica Wattman & David Farber
- *Start With Why* by Simon Sinek
- *Pre-Suasion* by Robert Cialdini

Conferences:
- Content Marketing World
- ScaleUp Summits by Gazelles Inc.
- Genius Network / 25k Group by Joe Polish
- Inbound by Hubspot
- Marketing Nation by Marketo
- The Adobe Summit

About the Author

Andy's thought leadership journey started when he published his first business book in 2007 and first magazines in 2009. Since that time, he has leveraged custom magazines and online digital content strategies to establish himself as a leading authority in content marketing and brand positioning. He is a regular contributor to PROFITguide.com.

Through his company, Carle Publishing Inc., Andy and his team make these strategies and tools accessible to their Client-Partners. They make creating a magazine and publishing online Easy, Effective and Economical.

CPSIA information can be obtained
at www.ICGtesting.com
Printed in the USA
FFOW03n1437070418
46187499-47437FF